What Kind of Dog Am I?

Written by

Kathleen DiMario and
Kelly DiMario

Illustrated by Emily Foster

A FRIEND OF POSHA

First Name

Last Name

Dedicated To The Memory of:

Grammy Joan
who would have loved her
Great-Granddogger, Posha

and

Dr. Eric Hudson
who truly loved all his patients

Copyright ©2014, Posha Books, LLC, 236 Washington St., Toms River NJ 08753
Posha The Rescued Dog Trademark of Posha Books LLC

Published by: Posha Books, LLC, 236 Washington St., Toms River NJ 08753

ISBN-13: 978-0692323946 (What Kind of Dog Am I)
ISBN-10: 0692323945

Visit us on the Web at www.PoshaTheRescuedDog.com

Hi! My name is Posha. I love going to the dog park with Kelly, my dog-mommy. She is my mommy now, because she rescued me from the dog shelter.

I love going to the dog park because I always meet new friends, like Doodle and Twinkle.

Sometimes I play with my friends. Sometimes I just play with my dog-sister Nikkers. We always have lots of fun.

But every time I go to the dog park, one of the other dog-mommies always asks my mommy, "What kind of dog is that?"

The other day, when my mommy was walking me, some man even yelled down from a ladder, "What kind of dog is that?"

I always think, "What a silly question!" I know I'm the kind of dog who has really different paws that turn out like a ballet dancer's feet.

I know I'm the kind of dog who hugs my mommy whenever she comes home because I am so happy to see her.

My dog-sister Nikkers
knows what kind of dog she
is. She's a French poodle.

When I ask her what kind
of dog I am she says,
"Je ne sais pas, Posha."
I think that's French for
"I don't know."

My mommy always tells them, "Posha is a rescued dog, but I think she is a Shih-Poo, a mixture of Shitzu and Poodle."

I always laugh because Shih-Poo is a really funny word.

It seems really weird to me because I don't know what "Shih-Poo" means. But I know what "rescued dog" means. I got picked by my mommy because she loved me right away.

But then the other dog-mommy sometimes says, "No, I think she is a Goldendoodle or a Westie."

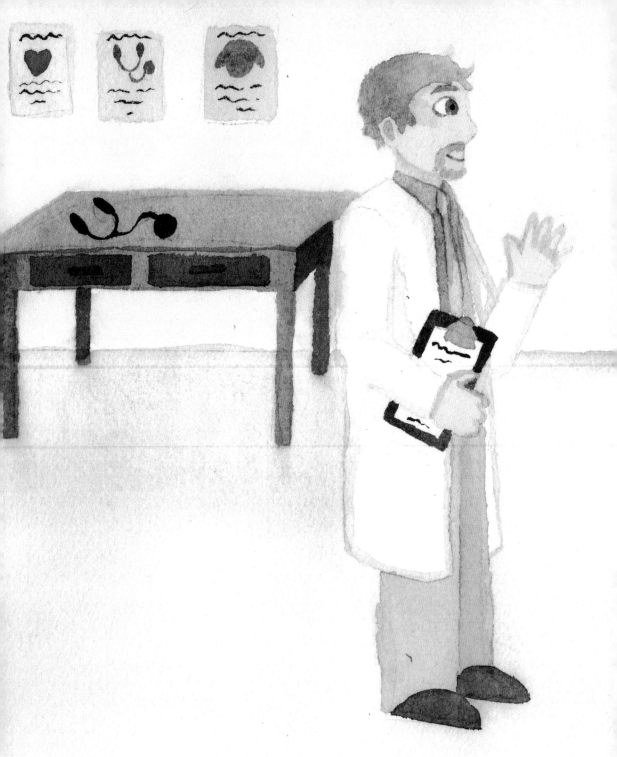

One day we went to an office and met a man who wore a white jacket. Mommy told me his name was "Dr. Hudson". She told me he was a veterinarian, which I think is a fancy word for doggy doctor.

She asked him, "Dr. Hudson, I need to know what kind of dog Posha is. Everyone always asks me, "What kind of dog is that?"

She looked really worried. I got so upset;
I licked her face to make her smile again.

Then Dr. Hudson said something that made her smile more than when I bring her Jed, my favorite toy dog.

Dr. Hudson said, "What does it matter what kind of dog Posha is?"

"All that matters is that you love her and she loves you. You are a family and that's what family means."

So we left Dr. Hudson's office and went to the dog park.

As soon as we got there, one of the other dog-mommies asked, "What kind of dog is that?"

My mommy smiled and said, "She's my Posha. She's the kind of dog that makes everyone who meets her happy. All that matters is that I love her, and she loves me."

That made me so happy.
I gave my mommy a big hug.

The End

LESSON LEARNED IN

"WHAT KIND OF DOG AM I?"

Posha is a rescued dog, so she doesn't know who her mommy and daddy are. Posha and her dog-mommy learn that the only thing that matters is that they love each other. So, like Posha, you know who you are by who loves you and who you love in return.